Discovering Biblical Treasures

UNDERSTANDING THE TEN COMMANDMENTS

A commentary using Ancient Bible Study Methods

Michael Harvey Koplitz

Acknowledgment

This work could not have been accomplished without Dr. Anne Davis, who taught me Ancient (Hebraic) Bible study methods, and my two study partners, Rev. Dr. Robert Cook, and Pastor Sandra Koplitz. We know that the journey has just started and will last a lifetime. The discovery of the depths of God's Word is waiting for us to find.

Michael H. Koplitz

TABLE OF CONTENTS

Introduction

The giving of the Ten Commandments was the event when the LORD revealed himself to Israel. Tradition says that the world fell silent. It was a pivotal moment in Israel's history. The people had to decide if they were going to accept the LORD's Torah. Midrash says that the universe would have ended on that day if Israel rejected the Torah. Also, it is believed that every Hebrew soul, past, present, and future were at the foot of Mount Sinai when the LORD spoke to Israel and gave them the Ten Commandments. It is an event in history that ties all Jewish people together.

It is believed that the people heard the LORD speaking these commandments. The

Mechilta[1] teaches that the LORD recited all Ten Commandments together in one utterance indicating that Israel heard all ten commandments.

The Sages taught that the word Torah, in Hebrew, equals the numeric value of 611 (using gematria[2]). Thus Moses taught the

---

[1] "The halakic midrash to Exodus. The name "Mekilta," which corresponds to the Hebrew "middah" (= "measure," "rule"), was given to this midrash because the Scriptural comments and explanations of the Law which it contains are based on fixed rules of Scriptural exegesis ("middot"; comp. Talmud Hermeneutics).' Source: http://www.jewishencyclopedia.com/articles/10594-mekilta

[2] "Gematria is a numerological system by which Hebrew letters correspond to numbers. This system, developed by practitioners of Kabbalah (Jewish mysticism), derived from Greek influence and became a tool for interpreting biblical texts. In gematria, each Hebrew letter is represented by a number (for example, aleph = 1, bet = 2, etc.). One can then calculate the numerical value of a word by adding together the values of each letter in it. In the realm of biblical interpretation, commentators base an argument on numerological equivalence of words. If a

people 611 of the 613 laws in the Torah. The other two laws are the first two commandments that the LORD taught the

---

word's numerical value equals that of another word, a commentator might draw a connection between these two words and the verses in which they appear and use this to prove larger conceptual conclusions." Source: https://www.myjewishlearning.com/article/gematria /

people directly. Rashi[3] and Ramban[4] believed that the Ten Commandments were uttered

---

[3] "Rashi, acronym **of** Rabbi Shlomo Yitzḥaqi, (born 1040, Troyes, Champagne—died July 13, 1105, Troyes), renowned medieval French commentator on the Bible and the Talmud (the authoritative Jewish compendium of law, lore, and commentary). Rashi combined the two basic methods of interpretation, literal and nonliteral, in his influential Bible commentary. His commentary on the Talmud was a landmark in Talmudic exegesis, and his work still serves among Jews as the most substantive introduction to biblical and postbiblical Judaism. Rashi also composed some penitential hymns (*seliḥot*), which revolve around twin themes: the harsh reality of exile and the comforting belief in redemption." Source: https://www.britannica.com/biography/Rashi

[4] "Nahmanides was a Spanish Talmudist, Kabbalist and biblical commentator (1194-1270), known, after the initial letters of his name, as Ramban (Rabbi Moshe ben Nahman). Nahmanides was born in Gerona, Spain, where he lived for most of his life. An outstanding Talmudist, his work in this field still enjoys the highest esteem among students of the Talmud. As a halachic authority, he exercised a great influence on the Codes of Jewish law, especially through the Responsa of his most distinguished disciple, Solomon Ibn Adret." Source:

from the LORD, but all the words were uttered at the same time. The people could not comprehend what the LORD said. So, the LORD repeated the commandments one word at a time. The people could not tolerate the intense holiness of this direct communication from the LORD and pleaded with Moses to teach them the rest of the commandments.[5]

> [22] "These words the LORD spoke to all your assembly at the mountain from the midst of the fire, *of* the cloud and *of* the thick gloom, with a great voice, and He added no more. He wrote them on two tablets of stone and gave them to me. [23] "And when you heard the voice from the midst of the darkness, while the mountain was burning with fire, you

---

https://www.myjewishlearning.com/article/nahmanides-ramban/

[5] Nosson Scherman, *The Chumash: the Torah: Haftaros and Five Megillos, with a Commentary Anthologized from the Rabbinic Writings* (Brooklyn, NY: Mesorah Publications, 1998).

came near to me, all the heads of your tribes and your elders. (Deut. 5:22-23 NAU)

The people heard the ten commandments from the LORD, but it was Moses who taught them eight of them.

The sage Gur Aryeh[6] said that the LORD gave all the commandments in one utterance to symbolize that Israel and the Torah are an

---

[6] "Four hundred years after his death, the Maharal of Prague remains a larger than life figure, just like his statue that stands in front of the Prague city hall. He was a bridge figure between worlds. He helped to close the gaps between the medieval period and the stirrings of modernity in the Enlightenment; between Torah and science; between philosophy and mysticism. Above all, he is appreciated for explicating the most difficult passages in the Aggada, making the intent of Chazal clear to the student intent on mining their deep wisdom from their sometimes obscure words." Source: https://torah.org/series/guraryeh/

inseparable unit. The Torah is not a collection of disparate commandments and statements. The Torah is one whole unified utterance from the LORD.

Why do we need to return to the original interpretation of the Word of God?

A personal story from the author: While I was attending Seminary earning my M. Div. degree, I started to question what the instructors and reference books were saying about the Scriptures. One of the ideas being offered then was that the Bible was full of errors and not factual. I found that attitude disturbing for Seminary instructors to be teaching. After all, the Seminary experience is to train pastors to go out into God's world and preach the Bible. How can you preach the Bible if you believe what these instructors are teaching? The methods that were being taught to examine the Bible just seemed inaccurate to me.

After graduating from Seminary, I spent much time reading different views about the Bible. I eventually read the Zohar. This collection of Midrashim is considered the secret work of the Torah, according to Kabbalists. Besides, I read quite a bit about Messianic Judaism. Their view of the Bible is quite different from the Seminary view.

I decided that the biblical interpretation that was being taught in Seminary was not the biblical interpretation the people heard when Jesus Christ (whose Hebraic name is Jesus) preached. I went on a quest to learn what the people of Jesus's day thought about Scripture, and what they thought when the Scriptures were read. This quest led me to Dr. Anne Davis and The Bible Learning University. Dr. Davis was in search of the same thing I was searching for. She had made many discoveries that helped me in my quest. I earned the Ph. D. degree from The Bible Learning University in Hebraic Studies in Christianity concentrating on ancient Bible Studies methods.

Finally, I found someone who believed that the church has placed almost 1900 years of their theological ideas about the Scriptures and in many places possibly distorting its original meaning. What is also important to hear is that the basic tenants of Jesus as God's Messiah, my Lord and Savior are in the Bible. My faith in Jesus is stronger now that I have learned from Dr. Davis how to study the Scriptures in the same manner that the people did in Jesus's day.

Our God is vast and infinite and so is His Word. May God bless you in your discovery of what God's Word is about.

How do people today in the church interpret Scripture? Generally speaking, the pastor or teacher of a Bible study class tells the members of the class what the Scripture means. Where are they getting their understanding? The answer is from the book they are using to teach the class. This is a Greek/western way of teaching. The book includes an article is in this book that describes the Greek/western way of teaching and learning.

So, where does our interpretation of Scripture come from? It started when the church decided to break away from its Hebraic roots around 60 CE. When the church became mainly Gentile, the desire to be connected to Judaism disappeared. There were political reasons for this separation and theological differences. The problem that arose is that the church learned how to interpret the Scriptures using the ways of the Greek philosophers, Plato, Aristotle, and Socrates. This style of learning is elegant for literature that was written in the Greek style.

However, Scripture is a Semitic document. Yes, even the New Testament is a Semitic document. Semitic authors wrote differently than Greek authors. The church used Greek methods to try to interpret the Scripture. By doing so, the church lost the original meaning of the Scripture.

How can we return to the original interpretation of Jesus' words? The first step is to acknowledge that Jesus was Jewish, his first disciples were Jewish, and the authors of the New Testament were Jewish. The second step is to learn how the authors of the Scripture wrote. The Hebraic methods of writing and interpreting Scripture has survived through the centuries and is being used today.

The Sage Hillel defined the Semitic way of Bible study. He lived approximately seventy-years before Jesus. By using Hillel's method and the Sages interpretations, we can discover the original interpretation of Jesus' words.

One other thing happened over the centuries to the interpretation of Jesus' words. For the first fifteen centuries the church leadership, pope, bishops and the like, determined what the Scripture meant. Using the Greek methodology of never challenging the teacher, the church interpretations of Scripture became fixed. The Reformation opened the door to new interpretations of the Scripture. Unfortunately, the Reformers used their Greek learning and teaching methods to interpret the Scripture. As each new denomination formed they accepted the interpretation of their founder as truth. Martin Luther said that the Scripture must be read literally. That statement brought about the Fundamentalist movement. The Scripture was not written literally. Therefore to read it literally does not offer the original meaning.

The Presbyterians follow George Whitfield's interpretation. The Lutherans follow Martin Luther's interpretation. The German Reformed follow John Calvin's interpretation. The Methodist denominations follow John Wesley's interpretation.

There are over 1900 years of filters that the church has put onto the Scripture. These filters have to be removed to obtain to the original meaning of the Scripture. That is what this book is all about. The student of the Scripture must learn to put aside everything the church has been teaching and look at the Scripture with fresh eyes. What does one look for? That question is answered in this book. The challenge is presented. It is up to you the student to determine what you will do with the tools and methodologies explained in this book. Several examples are included to help you on your path.

What is Ancient Bible Study Methods?

After 2000 years of Christian theology and thought, the original meaning to the Scriptures, especially the Christian Scriptures, have come to us today with a huge number of filters. These filters include the theological interpretations that have developed over the years about the meaning of the Scriptures. Unfortunately, Christianity divorced itself from its mother religion, Judaism, by the end of the first century C.E. By doing so, combined with the dwindling number of Jews in the church, the Hebraic understanding of the Scriptures was essentially lost and eventually considered invalid by the church

Bishops. Ignatius of Antioch (died in 107 C.E.) in his Epistle to the Magnesians wrote, "To profess Jesus Christ while continuing to follow Jewish customs is an absurdity. The Christian faith does not look to Judaism, but Judaism looks to Christianity."[7]

In addition to the filters, there is much cultural information not contained in the narratives of the Scriptures because the people of the Bible knew their own culture.

A modern example : If you were to write in your diary you went to church on Sunday, there would be a lot of information you would not include. Anyone reading your diary entry would know certain things intuitively. Some of these things would be (1) You drove your car;

---

[7] Friedman, David. *They Loved the Torah: What Jesus's First Followers Really Thought about the Law.* Baltimore, MD: Lederer Books, 2001. 10.

(2) The car had gasoline in it; (3) You had a driver's license; (4) You had paid for car insurance, just to list a few items. The same applies when the narratives of the Scriptures are read. When a narrative says that Jesus's disciples went into a field and picked grain, the narrator does not have to explain how grain was picked and how it was prepared for consumption. Another example would be the marriage story. The original listeners of the Scriptures did not need an explanation of what happened at a Jewish wedding. Read the account of Jesus at the wedding at Cana, and you will find there is a lot of cultural information left out about the ceremony and celebration because it was known by the people of the day.

So, to obtain a more complete understanding of the Scriptures, especially the words of Jesus, we need to learn how to think like a person did in Jesus's days. This can be done by combining the culture and customs of the people with a linguistic approach of the Scriptures. The people "listened" intently for the linguistic clues that led to depth of meaning because they did not have books or copies of the Scriptures to read. The Scriptures were passed down through the generations by a mouth to ear method.

Much has been written about the customs and manners of the ancient world, therefore, current research is sufficient. What makes this dissertation unique is that it is the combination of culture and to offer a Hebraic understanding of Scripture from Jesus's day as the Jewish listener heard it.

Dr. Robert Price makes an argument in his article <u>New Testament Narrative as Old Testament Midrash</u> that the New Testament is a retelling of the Old Testament, thus creating aggadah.[8] "The New Testament gospels and the Acts of the Apostles can be shown to be Christian aggadah upon Jewish scripture, and these narratives can be neither fully understood nor fully appreciated without tracing them to their underlying sources, the object of the present article."[9]

---

[8] Aggadah is "the non legal or narrative material, as parables, maxims, or anecdotes, in the Talmud and other rabbinical literature, serving either to illustrate the meaning or purpose of the law, custom, or Biblical passage being discussed or to introduce a different, unrelated topic." Source: "The Definition of Aggadah." *Dictionary.com*. N.p., n.d. Web. 1 Aug. 2016.

[9] Price, Robert M. "New Testament Narrative as Old Testament Midrash." In *The Christ-myth Theory and Its Problems*, 1. Cranford, NJ: American Atheist Press, 2011. Accessed August

What is the Greek system of learning? An overview of this system of learning is expressed by J. Parsons in his article <u>Theology and the Greek Mindset</u>. "The modern university, for example, was modeled after the ideals of Plato's Academy in which (it was hoped) the entire universe would be explained within its halls."[10] Today's Seminaries and Bible Colleges are part of the modern university system and therefore are using the learning methodology that Plato and his contemporaries used to view the universe. This system of learning and understanding is a part

---

01,   2016. http://www.robertmprice.mindvendor.com/art_midrash1.ht m.

[10] Parsons, John. "Theology and the Greek Mindset - a Brief Look." Theology and the Greek Mindset - a Brief Look. Accessed August 01, 2016. http://www.hebrew4christians.com/Articles/Hellenism/hel lenism.html.

of our current education system. Therefore, when teachers, who are considered experts in their field of study, instruct students, it is often frowned upon for the student to challenge the teacher or to create a debate when the student might not agree with the teacher's interpretation. In addition, the Greek method of learning calls the study of Scripture hermeneutics. Hermeneutics is "the science of interpretation, especially of the Scriptures."[11] This Greek approach is very different from the Hebraic method proposed by this study.

The learning methods of Socrates and his contemporaries make sense when studying, for example, "The Iliad" by Homer or other Greek philosophic documents, but these methods do not necessarily bring to life all of

____

[11] "Hermeneutics." Dictionary.com. Accessed April 14, 2016. http://dictionary.reference.com/browse/hermeneutics.

the flavors of ancient Middle Eastern documents. This Greek approach is the method of Bible study that has been employed by Christianity for over 1900 years.

Introducing the Ten Commandments

^{WTT} Exodus 20:1 וַיְדַבֵּר אֱלֹהִים אֵת כָּל־הַדְּבָרִים הָאֵלֶּה לֵאמֹר: ס ²אָנֹכִי֙ יְהוָה אֱלֹהֶיךָ אֲשֶׁר הוֹצֵאתִיךָ מֵאֶרֶץ מִצְרַיִם מִבֵּית עֲבָדִים:

^{NAU} **Exodus 20:1** Then God spoke all these words, saying, ² "I am the LORD your God, who brought you out of the land of Egypt, out of the house of slavery.

The Hebrew people had gone into Egypt when a famine struck the land of Canaan in the days of Jacob. His son Joseph was sold into slavery by ten of his brothers who were jealous that their father Jacob favored Joseph. While in Egypt, Joseph was able to rise to the rank of the viceroy of Egypt and was responsible for food distributions. His brothers came before him one day asking to purchase grain. They had a family reunion. The brothers returned to Canaan, and the family traveled to Egypt.

There was a time in Egyptian history that a Semitic dynasty existed in the Goshen area of Egypt. Joseph's rise to power was because the Pharaoh was a Semite at the time. The invitation to Joseph's family to come to Egypt and being settled in Goshen supports this idea. Goshen was in the Nile delta region and was very fertile. The Hebrew people thrived and proliferated in this area.

The Semitic dynasty came to an end. What was the new Pharoah going to do with the large population of Hebrew people in Goshen? The solution was to enslave the people. By doing so, the Pharoah was able to advert a revolution by the Semitic people in Egypt. It also gave him a large workforce.

The Hebrew people never forgot about the God of Abraham, Isaac, and Jacob. They had not experienced a revelation of the LORD while they were in Egypt until the redeemer came. Moses, the redeemer, directed the power of the LORD against Egypt and was able to free the slaves.

The Exodus from Egypt and the reception of the Ten Commandments is the defining moment for the Hebrew people. The people traveled through the Red Sea and made their way to Mount Sinai. This mountain had been considered the mountain of God for many years. Moses met an angel of the LORD at the Burning Bush on Mount

Sinai. The time had come for all of Israel to meet the LORD.

The Ten Commandments commence with a positive commandment that the people must believe in the LORD who brought them out of slavery. It is written in the Mechilta that a conquering king entered his new domain and the populace asked him to pronounce his decrees. He responded, "First, you must accept my sovereignty; only then can I set forth my decrees." The LORD was saying to Israel that she had to accept the sovereignty of the LORD before they would receive His laws.[12]

---

[12] Nosson Scherman, *The Chumash: the Torah: Haftaros and Five Megillos, with a Commentary Anthologized from the Rabbinic Writings* (Brooklyn, NY: Mesorah Publications, 1998).

יְהֹוָה

This word is usually translated as "I am the LORD your God."

This is the name of God that Moses received at the Burning Bush. In most English Bible translations it is translated as "the LORD." Usually, the actual name of God is capitalized. This is the name of God that the High Priest would say once a year on Yom Kippur in the Temple at Jerusalem. The High Priest would be in front of the Ark of the Covenant when he said that name. Unfortunately, with the destruction of the Second Temple in Jerusalem, the name was never spoken again. The pronunciation of the name was lost. Hebrew does not have written vowels thus the loss of the pronunciation. Yahweh may be the correct pronunciation, but this will never be known. Therefore, this phrase could be translated as "I am Yahweh your God."

"who brought you out of the land of Egypt, out of the house of slavery."

Why would the LORD have to identify Himself to the people? The Sage Rashi suggests that since the LORD does not have a body that it was difficult for the people to perceive the LORD's essence. Our understanding of the LORD is defined on how the LORD manifests himself. In Egypt, the Hebrew people experienced the LORD as a mighty warrior. At Sinai, the LORD was a compassionate Father.[13]

The Zohar[14] explains that the LORD redeemed the people at the forty-ninth and next to the absolute lowest possible level of spiritual contamination. This is why the Exodus is mentioned numerous times in the Torah and in connection with the many commandments.[15]

---

[13] IBID.

[14] "The Zohar (Hebrew זֹהַר; Splendor, radiance) is widely considered the most important work of Kabbalah, Jewish mysticism. It is a mystical commentary on the Torah (five books of Moses), written in medieval Aramaic and medieval Hebrew. It contains a mystical discussion of the nature of God, the origin and structure of the universe, the nature of souls, sin, redemption, good and evil, and related topics. The Zohar is not one book, but a group of books. These books include scriptural interpretations as well as material on theosophic theology, mythical cosmogony, mystical psychology, and what some would call anthropology." Source: https://www.jewishvirtuallibrary.org/the-zohar

[15] IBID.

The FIRST Commandment

^{WTT} **Exodus 20:3** לֹא יִהְיֶה־לְךָ֣ אֱלֹהִ֥ים אֲחֵרִ֖ים עַל־פָּנָֽי׃

^{NAU} **Exodus 20:3** "You shall have no other gods before Me.

The LORD is the creator of Heaven and Earth. There is no other God. This is a foundational stone of the Hebrew people and a statement of their faith in the LORD. Their devotion to the LORD as the one and only God of Heaven and Earth makes them an outstanding people. This faith in the LORD is what kept them alive throughout the centuries of persecution and severe suffering. Many people have tried to destroy the

Hebrew people. The people's faith that the LORD would ensure that a remnant of the people always survived is a significant factor in the faith.

The LORD is a spiritual Deity. The LORD is God from everlasting to everlasting. He is the creator and sole ruler of the Universe. The LORD does not share this action, unlike the pagan gods of the tribes and nations of the ancient world.

עַל-פָּנָֽי

This phrase raises a different translation than is usually found in the English versions of the Bible. It can be translated as "above my face." To be "above my face" means to be in the presence. "My presence" means forever. Since the LORD is eternal, then this commandment is eternal. Therefore, another translation can be:

"You shall not recognize the gods of others in My presence."

From the English translation, "no other gods" implies that the Hebrew people at Sinai did not believe in monotheism. The Hebrew people believed that their God, Yahweh, was the sole creator of Heaven and Earth. In ancient times it was believed that every nation had their god(s) that took care of them. It was believed that nations went to war on Earth because a holy war broke out between rival gods. The full understanding of monotheism does not come until the Babylon Exile period. The book of Jonah states that the

LORD is God over all nations. Jonah is sent by the LORD to warn the Ninevites that punishment was coming to them because of their bad ethics, morals, and sins. Jonah tries to run from the LORD. It was believed that the LORD resided inside the borders of the Northern and Southern Kingdoms of Israel. Jonah quickly discovered that the LORD is everywhere when the storm hit the boat he was on.

The alternate translation demonstrates this inherent belief of the time. The LORD told the people that to recognize any other god was unacceptable. It is a statement of monotheism and it recognizes the people's understanding. The people spent 270 years in Egypt. During that time they learned about the various Egyptian deities. It would take time for the Hebrew people to come to a full understanding of what monotheism is.

The SECOND Commandment

לֹא תַעֲשֶׂה־לְךָ פֶסֶל֙ וְכָל־תְּמוּנָ֗ה אֲשֶׁ ר בַּשָּׁמַיִם֙ מִמַּעַל וַאֲשֶׁר֙ בָּאָרֶץ מִתָּ חַת וַאֲשֶׁ ר בַּמַּ֣יִם׀ מִתַּ֣חַת לָאָרֶץ: ⁵לֹא־תִשְׁתַּחְוֶ֥ה לָהֶם֙ וְלֹא תָעָבְדֵ֑ם כִּ֣י אָנֹכִ֞י יְהוָ֤ה אֱלֹהֶ֙יךָ֙ אֵ֣ל קַנָּ֔א פֹּקֵ֨ד עֲוֺ֧ן אָבֹ֛ת עַל־ בָּנִ֥ים עַל־שִׁלֵּשִׁים וְעַל־רִבֵּעִים לְשֹׂנְאָ֑י: ⁶וְעֹ֥שֶׂה חֶ֙סֶד֙ לַאֲלָפִ֔ים לְאֹהֲבַ֖י וּלְשֹׁמְרֵ֥י מִצְוֺתָֽי: ס

⁴ "You shall not make for yourself an idol, or any likeness of what is in heaven above or on the earth beneath or in the water under the earth. ⁵ "You shall not worship them or serve them; for I, the LORD your God, am a jealous God, visiting the iniquity of the fathers on the children, on the third and the fourth generations of those who hate Me, ⁶ but showing lovingkindness to thousands, to those who love Me and keep My commandments.

This commandment has the most explanation associated with it. Ancient people worshiped images and idols of their deities. The idols were made of wood, silver, gold, and stone. The gods of ancient peoples were human deities. Humans rose to the rank of deities because of their power, wealth, being heroes, kings, princes, and holy men. Many of the gods of ancient times have been lost to antiquity, however many of their images are available today, and people seek out these idols today.[16]

The sun, moon, and the planets were worshiped as gods and temples were erected to allow the people to worship them. Over the centuries as humans tried to find God, they even worshiped animals, trees, brooks, fish,

---

[16] Rocco A. Errico and George M. Lamsa, *Aramaic Light on Exodus through Deuteronomy: a Commentary Based on the Aramaic Language and Ancient Near Eastern Customs* (Smyrna, GA: Noohra Foundation, Inc., 2008).

and other creatures. This commandment makes it clear that human deities, the lights in the sky nor the animals and plants on the Earth were god.

Ancient people would hold processions and feasts to their deities. Many times people argued and fought each other in an attempt to elevate their deity. They would argue over which god was born first.

Our God is a spiritual deity. One cannot see God. Therefore, one cannot portray Him with any image or idol. Over time even the pagan religions came to acknowledge that there was one deity that created Heaven and Earth. However, they kept their deities as intermediaries and intercessors between humans and the creator of Heaven and Earth. Every tribe and nation had their deities that they paid homage to, and they believed that the deity would speak to the creator for them.

תַעֲשֶׂה־לְךָ פֶּסֶל (Exod. 20:4 WTT)

This phrase is translated as "make yourself an idol." It can also be translated as "make yourself something hewed." As noted early, in ancient times metal, wood or stone would be hewed into an image of an idol. Not only was the LORD saying not to have idols He also said do not make idols. There were Hebrews who probably made idols for the surrounding tribes because it was a form of income. However, this commandment not only forbids the Hebrews from worshiping such idols it also prevents them from making them for other people.

וְכָל־תְּמוּנָ֡ה (Exod. 20:4 WTT)

This phrase means "or any likeness." The ban against making idols for Israel or any other tribe is further inforced by the repetition of the ban to manufacture idols.

בָּאָ֫רֶץ מִתַּ֫חַת וַאֲשֶׁ֫ר בַּמַּ֫יִם׀ מִתַּ֫חַת לָאָֽרֶץ (Exod. 20:4 WTT)

This phrase is translated as "on the earth beneath or in the water under the earth." This phrase makes it inclusive that anything that grows on the Earth, any animal on the Earth, and everything that is in the oceans cannot be worshiped as a deity. This covers the ancient tribal belief that the plants, earthly animals, and water-based animals cannot be considered deities.

קַנָּ֔א (Exod. 20:5 WTT)

This word is usually translated as "jealous." It can be translated as "zealous" or " impassioned." There are two places in the Hebrew Scripture that this word refers to "jealous." This verse and in Numbers 5:14 which refers to a suspicious husband's claim that his wife was unfaithful, it means abuse of trust and someone's refusal to give up something that is rightfully his.

In this verse, referring to idolatry, it means that God alone is entitled to the veneration of humans and will not stand for the countenance worship to other false gods. The Mechilta reads that God says, "For idolatry, I zealously exact punishment, but in other matters, I am gracious and merciful."[17]

---

[17] Nosson Scherman, *The Chumash: the Torah: Haftaros and Five Megillos, with a Commentary Anthologized from the*

פֹּקֵד עֲוֹן אָבֹת עַל־בָּנִים עַל־שִׁלֵּשִׁים וְעַל־רִבֵּעִים לְשֹׂנְאָ֑י

(Exod. 20:5 WTT)

This phrase is translated as "visiting the iniquity of the fathers on the children, on the third and the fourth generations of those who hate Me." How can children be punished for the behavior of their parents? The Sages tell us that the children can be punished for the sins of their parents if they continue to sin in the same manner. This creates a legacy and when the sin is repeated throughout several generations then the sin can become a legitimate part of the society's culture and a way of life. Thus a new pattern of behavior is established. Sins are not acceptable to the

---

Rabbinic Writings (Brooklyn, NY: Mesorah Publications, 1998).

LORD even if the culture accepts the sin as a part of its overall laws and behavior.[18]

וְעֹשֶׂה חֶסֶד לַאֲלָפִים לְאֹהֲבַי וּלְשֹׁמְרֵי מִצְוֺתָי (Exod. 20:6 WTT)

This phrase is translated as "but showing lovingkindness to thousands, to those who love Me and keep My commandments." It means that the LORD will find kindness to at least two thousand generations who keep His laws and these commandments.

---

[18] IBID.

The THIRD Commandment

לֹא תַעֲשֶׂה־לְךָ פֶּסֶל וְכָל־תְּמוּנָה אֲשֶׁר בַּשָּׁמַיִם ׀ ⁴
מִמַּעַל וַאֲשֶׁר בָּאָרֶץ מִתָּחַת וַאֲשֶׁר בַּמַּיִם ׀ מִתַּחַת
לָאָרֶץ: (Exod. 20:4 WTT)

⁷ "You shall not take the name of the LORD your God in vain, for the LORD will not leave him unpunished who takes His name in vain. (Exod. 20:7 NAU)

What does it mean to take the name of God in vain? To do this, the word שָׁוְא (Exod. 20:7 WTT) must be examined. In principal English translations of the Scripture, this word is translated as "in vain." It means "vanity" or "falsehood." For this commandment, the translation "falsehood" is fitting. This commandment comes from the method that merchants and buyers were using. A negotiation for the price of an object would occur between a buyer and seller. Prices were not marked on items. Instead, a negotiating of price occurred. The merchant would start at a high price. The buyer would refuse to pay such a price. The merchant might lower the price and invoke the name of the LORD. The buyer would also invoke the name of the LORD when a counteroffer was made. The buyer would invoke the name of his son, swear on the graves of his ancestors, for the merchant to give him the actual price. Through bargaining over goods the name of the LORD was used to cheat and deceive.[19]

____

[19] Rocco A. Errico and George M. Lamsa, *Aramaic Light on Exodus through Deuteronomy: a Commentary Based on the Aramaic Language and Ancient Near Eastern Customs* (Smyrna, GA: Noohra Foundation, Inc., 2008).

The Targum Onkelos[20] translates the first part of the commandment as: "Thou shalt not swear in the name of the Lord thy God vainly." This translation corresponds to the usage of the LORD's name in business transactions.

כִּי לֹא יְנַקֶּה יְהוָה אֵת אֲשֶׁר־יִשָּׂא אֶת־שְׁמוֹ לַשָּׁוְא

(Exod. 20:7 WTT)

---

[20] During the period when the Jews suffered bitterly under the rule of the hated Emperor Hadrian who quelled the uprising of Bar Kochba, razed the great city of Bethar and murdered many Jews, among them Rabbi Akivah (approximately in the year 3880, 52 years after the destruction of the second Beth Hamikdosh), there arose a bright star that lights up the Jewish heavens even to this day. We are referring to the great Onkelos, who translated the Torah into Aramaic, a translation (which is also an interpretation) known as "Targum Onkelos." It is printed almost in every Chumash. "Targum Onkelos" is so holy that when one reviews the weekly portion (as one is supposed to do every week) it has to be reviewed twice in the Chumash and once in Targum. Source: https://www.chabad.org/library/article_cdo/aid/112286/jewish/Onkelos.htm

This phrase is usually translated as "for the LORD will not leave him unpunished, who takes His name in vain." A closer translation to the original Hebrew is "for the LORD will not clear one who swears falsely by His name. (Exod. 20:7 TNK)" When a person swears an oath and uses the LORD's name, the person is saying that his/her word is as right as the LORD's existence. If the oath is violated the person who made the oath is holding the LORD in contempt. In doing so the LORD will never absolve the person.[21]

---

[21] Nosson Scherman, *The Chumash: the Torah: Haftaros and Five Megillos, with a Commentary Anthologized from the Rabbinic Writings* (Brooklyn, NY: Mesorah Publications, 1998).

The FORTH Commandment

זָכוֹר֙ אֶת־י֣וֹם הַשַּׁבָּ֔ת לְקַדְּשֽׁוֹ׃ ⁹ שֵׁ֤שֶׁת יָמִים֙ תַּֽעֲבֹ֔ד וְעָשִׂ֖יתָ כָּל־מְלַאכְתֶּֽךָ׃ ¹⁰ וְי֙וֹם֙ הַשְּׁבִיעִ֔י שַׁבָּ֖ת ׀ לַיהוָ֣ה אֱלֹהֶ֑יךָ לֹֽא־תַעֲשֶׂ֣ה כָל־מְלָאכָ֡ה אַתָּ֣ה ׀ וּבִנְךָֽ־וּבִתֶּ֡ךָ עַבְדְּךָ֩ וַאֲמָתְךָ֙ וּבְהֶמְתֶּ֔ךָ וְגֵרְךָ֖ אֲשֶׁ֥ר בִּשְׁעָרֶֽיךָ׃ ¹¹ כִּ֣י שֵֽׁשֶׁת־יָמִים֩ עָשָׂ֨ה יְהוָ֜ה אֶת־הַשָּׁמַ֣יִם וְאֶת־הָאָ֗רֶץ אֶת־הַיָּם֙ וְאֶת־כָּל־אֲשֶׁר־בָּ֔ם וַיָּ֖נַח בַּיּ֣וֹם הַשְּׁבִיעִ֑י עַל־כֵּ֗ן בֵּרַ֧ךְ יְהוָ֛ה אֶת־י֥וֹם הַשַּׁבָּ֖ת וַֽיְקַדְּשֵֽׁהוּ׃ ס

(Exod. 20:8-11 WTT)

⁸ "Remember the sabbath day, to keep it holy. ⁹ "Six days you shall labor and do all your work, ¹⁰ but the seventh day is a sabbath of the LORD your God; *in it* you shall not do any work, you or your son or your daughter, your male or your female servant or your cattle or your sojourner who stays with you. ¹¹ "For in six days the LORD made the heavens and the earth, the sea and all that is in them, and rested on the seventh day; therefore the LORD blessed the sabbath day and made it holy.

(Exod. 20:8-11 NAU)

The observance of the sabbath is a foundational stone of the Hebraic religion. During the time of Yeshua the Messiah of Nazareth, Sabbath observance was the most important of the Ten Commandments. Vast commentaries detailing strict and rigid observance of the sabbath were written. The day was supposed to be a time for people to be free from all the toils and work of the masses so that they would be with their families and worship the LORD.

The sabbath day was changed to Sunday by Emperor Constantine for Christianity. The Council of Laodicea in 360 CE changed the date. The Emperor made himself the guardian of the faith.[22] By doing so he could change any aspect of Christianity that he wished.

In modern times the Sabbath is a time for prayer, fasting and good works. The Sabbath reminds us that the LORD is the creator of Heaven and Earth. It also reminds us that the LORD spent six days creating Heaven and Earth, and He rested on the seventh day. The Sabbath is to be sanctified by wearing beautiful clothing, eating excellent food, and devoting the day to the study of the Scripture and in service to the LORD.[23]

---

[22] Rocco A. Errico and George M. Lamsa, *Aramaic Light on Exodus through Deuteronomy: a Commentary Based on the Aramaic Language and Ancient Near Eastern Customs* (Smyrna, GA: Noohra Foundation, Inc., 2008).

[23] Nosson Scherman, *The Chumash: the Torah: Haftaros and Five Megillos, with a Commentary Anthologized from the Rabbinic Writings* (Brooklyn, NY: Mesorah Publications, 1998).

זָכֹור (Exod. 20:8 WTT)

This word means "to remember." "It also implies repentance (see Ezek 6:9) or observing the commandments (see Num 15:40) especially that of the Sabbath (Exo 20:8). "For the ends of the earth, remembrance is repentance" (Psa 22:27). In political relations, not remembering a treaty is to break it (see Amos 1:9). Such cases are clear examples of distinct causes and effects, but in some other cases the relation between the remembering and the joint action is so close that they are virtually identified in the mind of the writer."[24]

A part of the sanctification of the Sabbath is to repent for any sins that have been committed. If this is done every week on the

---

[24] R. Laird Harris, Gleason L. Archer, and Bruce K. Waltke, *Theological Wordbook of the Old Testament* (Chicago: Moody Press, 2004).

Sabbath then repentance would be for the week and the soul would be cleansed.

The FIFTH Commandment

כַּבֵּד אֶת־אָבִיךָ וְאֶת־אִמֶּךָ לְמַעַן יַאֲרִכוּן יָמֶיךָ עַל הָאֲדָמָה אֲשֶׁר־יְהוָה אֱלֹהֶיךָ נֹתֵן לָךְ׃ ס(Exod. 20:12 WTT)

[12] "Honor your father and your mother, that your days may be prolonged in the land which the LORD your God gives you. (Exod. 20:12 NAU)

In the Near East, family ties were essential and were preserved for a long time. It was not unusual for children to live with their parents under the same roof. It was a sacred duty to care for parents. Besides, children would seek out the wisdom and counsel from their parents. In return, their parents offered blessings and guidance to their children.[25]

The Sages believed that when honoring one's parent that one was honoring the LORD. Having respect for parents is a part of one's obligation to the LORD.[26]

כַּבֵּד אֶת־אָבִיךָ וְאֶת־אִמֶּךָ (Exod. 20:12 WTT)

This phrase is translated as "honor your father and mother." What does it mean to pay honor? The first word of the phrase can be

---

[25] Rocco A. Errico and George M. Lamsa, *Aramaic Light on Exodus through Deuteronomy: a Commentary Based on the Aramaic Language and Ancient Near Eastern Customs* (Smyrna, GA: Noohra Foundation, Inc., 2008).

[26] Nosson Scherman, *The Chumash: the Torah: Haftaros and Five Megillos, with a Commentary Anthologized from the Rabbinic Writings* (Brooklyn, NY: Mesorah Publications, 1998).

translated as "be heavy, grievous, hard, rich, honorable, or glorious."[27]

To honor parents refers to deeds that raise the status of parents or provide them with comfort if necessary, which would include food, drink, clothing, and shelter. A child is not permitted to do anything that would disgrace or degrade their parents.

Children who have abusive parents might find it difficult, if not impossible, to honor their parents. The Sages connect the tenth commandment about coveting with the fifth commandment about honoring parents. The Mechilta connects the two by saying that a covetous parent will have children who dishonor them, because the parent's selfishness

---

[27] R. Laird Harris, Gleason L. Archer, and Bruce K. Waltke, *Theological Wordbook of the Old Testament* (Chicago: Moody Press, 2004).

can lead them to overstep all bounds of decent conduct, putting selfish desires above all other considerations.[28]

Another view of abusive parents is that their abusiveness indicates that they are not spiritual people and do not hold the LORD in reverence. Children are a blessing from the LORD. Abusive parents do not view children as blessings but rather as curses. When a parent views a blessing from the LORD as a curse, then they are not obeying the Word of the LORD. This type of person turns to the negative side of the Universe and can become overtaken by Satan because of their evil ways. It is against the Laws of the LORD to honor

---

[28] Nosson Scherman, *The Chumash: the Torah: Haftaros and Five Megillos, with a Commentary Anthologized from the Rabbinic Writings* (Brooklyn, NY: Mesorah Publications, 1998).

any person who has become a part of the Kingdom of Satan. Therefore, the children would be exempt from this commandment until their abusive parents leave the Kingdom of Satan, repent, and return to the ways of the LORD because one must not honor Satan or his evil demons.

The SIXTH Commandment

[WTT] לָא תִּרְצָ֖ח׃ ס **Exodus 20:13**

[NAU] **Exodus 20:13** "You shall not murder.

A person who believes in the LORD and His Word would not commit murder. The LORD is the creator and sustainer of life. It is for the LORD to create souls and life and for the LORD to destroy souls or cause death.[29]

When this commandment was given to the Hebrew people, every nation had its gods, laws, and ordinances. Therefore, this law meant that a member of the Hebrew tribe was not permitted to kill any other member of the tribe. During the travels in the wilderness,

---

[29] IBID.

Moses instructed the people to kill the men and women of Midian. Moses issued this order because Midian was attacking Israel. Therefore, going to war against an enemy who is trying to kill you is not considered murder. When the LORD as the creator of Heaven and Earth is accepted as universal, in the eighth century B.C.E.[30] the Ten Commandments and other Laws which the LORD gave to the Hebrew people became law throughout the Near East.

---

[30] Rocco A. Errico and George M. Lamsa, *Aramaic Light on Exodus through Deuteronomy: a Commentary Based on the Aramaic Language and Ancient Near Eastern Customs* (Smyrna, GA: Noohra Foundation, Inc., 2008).

The SEVENTH Commandment

WTT Exodus 20:14 לֹא תִּנְאָף: ס

NAU **Exodus 20:14** "You shall not commit adultery.

This command refers to the sacredness of marriage and family ties. In Genesis, it reads that a man will leave his parents to cleave with this wife. This commandment against committing adultery creates the sacredness of marriage. When Pharoah learned that he was going to marry Abraham's wife Sarah, Pharaoh immediately returned her to him. Morality was influential among the peoples in the Near East.[31]

The Mechilta says that someone who betrays the marital relationship can be expected to betray the LORD. The violation of this commandment is a capital offense if the offender is cohabitating with a married woman. The Sages created different levels of offenses for this commandment.[32]

"Adultery (sexual intercourse between a married woman and a man other than her husband [the biblical prohibition does not include sex between a married man and an unmarried woman]) is the only sexual offense recorded in the Ten Commandments. It is

---

[31] IBID.

[32] Nosson Scherman, *The Chumash: the Torah: Haftaros and Five Megillos, with a Commentary Anthologized from the Rabbinic Writings* (Brooklyn, NY: Mesorah Publications, 1998).

again recorded in the "Holiness Code" of Leviticus. The Book of Genesis calls adultery "the great sin" and the Talmud calls adultery *ha'averah* (the sin par excellence). According to rabbinic tradition, it [along with incest, in the category of *gilui arayot*] is considered one of the three sins (along with idolatry and murder) that people should avoid even at the pain of death. The gravity of adultery is evident by the fact that the Bible describes the offense as being punishable by the death penalty for both the man and the woman."[33]

---

[33] Ronald H. Isaacs, "Adultery," My Jewish Learning (My Jewish Learning, February 21, 2003), Accessed September 19, 2019 https://www.myjewishlearning.com/article/adultery/.

The EIGHT Commandment

[WTT] לֹא תִּגְנֹב׃ ס **Exodus 20:15**

[NAU] **Exodus 20:15** "You shall not steal.

This commandment refers explicitly to kidnapping.[34] It also refers to a kidnapping where the victim is forced to work for the kidnapper, and then the victim is sold into slavery.[35]

The definition of stealing, not being kidnapping, is found in the book of Leviticus.

---

[34] R. Laird Harris, Gleason L. Archer, and Bruce K. Waltke, *Theological Wordbook of the Old Testament* (Chicago: Moody Press, 2004).

[35] Nosson Scherman, *The Chumash: the Torah: Haftaros and Five Megillos, with a Commentary Anthologized from the Rabbinic Writings* (Brooklyn, NY: Mesorah Publications, 1998).

^{NAU} **Leviticus 19:11** 'You shall not steal, nor deal falsely, nor lie to one another. (Lev. 19:11 NAU)

The NINTH Commandment

^{WTT} **Exodus 20:16** לֹא־תַעֲנֶה בְרֵעֲךָ עֵד שָׁקֶר׃ ס

^{NAU} **Exodus 20:16** "You shall not bear false witness against your neighbor.

This command means that in front of a judge only the truth can be spoken. This passage also prohibits gossip and slander. "The Sages apply it to prohibit testimony even in cases where a witness is convinced that something took place but he did not actually see it."[36]

This commandment is parallel to the fourth commandment about violating the Sabbath. The Sabbath is a testimony that the

---

[36] IBID.

LORD created the Heavens and Earth in six days. It is believed that if a person can lie in a court of law, then that person can come to deny the LORD as the Creator of Heaven and Earth.[37]

---

[37] IBID.

The TENTH Commandment

WTT **Exodus 20:17** לֹא תַחְמֹד בֵּית רֵעֶךָ לֹא־
תַחְמֹד אֵשֶׁת רֵעֶךָ וְעַבְדּוֹ וַאֲמָתוֹ וְשׁוֹרוֹ וַחֲמֹרוֹ וְכֹל
אֲשֶׁר לְרֵעֶךָ׃ פ

NAU **Exodus 20:17** "You shall not covet your neighbor's house; you shall not covet your neighbor's wife or his male servant or his female servant or his ox or his donkey or anything that belongs to your neighbor."

A peasant of a kingdom could never draw his lust to the queen. It would never happen. A peasant could lust after his neighbor's daughter because this lust could be satisfied. A logical person realizes that desiring something or someone which is not possible will not attempt to gain such a prize. Unfortunately, that is not always true. A person who is a true disciple of the LORD would realize that there is a reason that the LORD does not want that person to possess something that his/her neighbor has.[38]

Covetousness is a form of lust because it takes over the person into wanting something that is not theirs. Covetousness tends to lead one to other crimes, such as theft and murder. Not lusting over what a neighbor has is the best way to prevent any offenses against the Laws of the LORD.

There are biblical narratives about what covetousness can do. There is a narrative about King Ahab who coveted a field and what happened when he could not buy it at first.

---

[38] IBID.

There is a narrative about what happened to King David when he lusted for Bathsheba.

Conclusion

When examining the Ten Commandments in its original language and connecting the ancient culture of the Near East, the original meaning is discovered. Over the years the Ten Commandments were read and obeyed by a literal interpretation. The literal reading of the Ten Commandments using Western/Greek analysis is what takes away the original meaning. Applying Ancient Bible Study Methods brings back the original meaning.

The Ten Commandments in its original form applies to any society in any age. Instead of removing the Ten Commandments from public places, society should be educating its people about their intentions. The world would be a better place if all people would follow the Word of the LORD.

Bibliography

2003. *Adultery.* February 21. Accessed September 19, 2019.
https://www.myjewishlearning.com/article/adultery/.

Friedman, David. 2001. *They Loved the Torah: What Jesus' first followers Really thought about the Law.* Baltimore, MD: Lederer Books.

Harris, Robert Laird. 1981. *Theological Word Book of the Old Testament.*

n.d. *Hermeneutics.* Accessed April 14, 2016.
http://dictionary.reference.com/browse/hermeneutics.

Parsons, John. n.d. *Theology and Greek Mindset Set.* Accessed August 01, 2016.
http://www.hebrew4christians.com/Articles/Hellenism/hellenism.html.

Price, Robert. n.d. *New Testament Narrative as Old Testament Midrash.* Accessed August 01, 2016.
http://www.robertmprice.mindvendor.com/art_midrash1.htm.

Scherman, Nosson. 1998. *The Chumash: The Torah: Haftaros and Five Megillos.* Brooklyn, NY: Mesorah Publications.